THE SECRET PLACE

FROM YOUTH TO ADULTHOOD

By

BONAVENTURA APICELLA

Copyright © by Bonaventura Apicella

All rights reserved. No part of this publication may be reproduced, distributed or transmitted in any form or mechanical methods, without the prior written permission of the publisher. For permission requests write to the author via the email below.

Email: bonares@talktalk.net

Content

- Preface..
- Introduction...
- Teenagers...
- Summer school holidays...........................
- Looking for work.....................................
- The secret place.......................................

Preface

All the names of friends used in this book have been changed to protect and respect family privacy.

Since my younger days, when I was a teenager, I have grown up like everybody else in this big world of ours where if one is not careful, they will cut their own life short by the way they choose to live their lives, and the crowd they associate themselves with, which will either become a blessing for them or a curse.

We have one life here on this earth, and it's not about getting very rich that is important (as many do) although money is important, we are not to let money become our idol, the boss, the pull in all and for all, for it will slowly but surely rule us, it will take charge in our hearts, spirits, soul and body, it will blind us to the things that are more important, and in the course of our lives we will hurt people and those close to us, and most of all, even if it isn't believed or understood or conceived to be so, we will hurt ourselves the most.

Whether people are in agreement with this or not, it isn't the real issue, what matters is to see ahead where we are going and for what reason, what meaning and purpose has this one life here on earth and whether we know or not how we are built, how we are constructed and not just in the flesh and blood, but in our inner selves, that is our spirit and soul and how these affect our hearts and minds, and consequently our bodies, decisions (good and bad) our health and well being too. Many believe that we are also spiritual beings and many do not. Generally, we are accustomed to believe only in what we see or can touch. This is what we normally learn to trust in as life goes on and we are very unsure of what we cannot see or can not touch. We can see on an operating table everything inside of us been exposed and it can be touched, but our soul and spirit, although they exist inside of us too they are invisible and cannot be touched, and this is why many are sceptical on this subject.

It is also true to say that pollution in this world is affecting all of us in our health and stability, everything is growing in every industry at a faster rate as it is with the growth of the world's population, which in turn produces more motorbikes, cars, vans, agricultural machines, construction machines, lorries, boats, vessels, ships, planes, helicopters, missiles, bombs, dirty chemicals, atomic and toxic tests going on here and there, forest trees are been logged more and more, and the balance of our earthly nature will one day give way to this relentless onslaught, particularly with the continuous extraction of natural oils, minerals such as copper, zinc, naming a few and all the fuel material being extracted from the earth, and who knows what else is been done below us. When (not if) nature will hit back at us it will be nothing like the natural disasters we have experienced so far in our history and the yesterdays of late (except Noah's flood of course). It is going to be of a catastrophic magnitude that will affect and drastically reshape the entire earth landscapes, seas and even the constellations above. I give you a little example. What happens when some mechanical engine parts that need grease and lubrication, say once a month, begin to be greased less and less, like once every three months, and later on, every four months, and so on up the scale of numbers, till one day those parts will be so dry and so worn in parts due to no grease or lubrication that when they will rub against each other they will suddenly give a might clunking and everything will shake and explode and fall apart. Do you see this happening in the tectonic plates of the earth one day? I do. Mother earth has been violated, taken advantage of, abused and downtrodden from the air, from the ground and from intrusions in the bases of her foundations, and one day she is going to release her anger at those who have caused her much distress and ill treatment, with the biggest earthquake mankind has ever seen, has ever been recorded or can ever be imagined to happen. But back to the secret place in question is it on earth somewhere? No. Is it in the underground or the space above or beneath the waters? No. So where is this secret place? Answer: it is inside of us and it will shape our life, our living with fellow human beings and our future days here on earth. Keep reading to find out.

Introduction

The purpose of this book is to open our eyes to the core truth of faith and spirit and learn to live and be in touch with these two invisible forms that have strength, power and life, more than our muscles. Once our bodies cease to live and die and are no more, faith, spirit and soul will go on living forever, but where will they go? So, for our good and the good of those near us, around us and far from us, for the sake of our children and grandchildren, and before it is too late for the entire world population, let us learn to live in harmony with our inner self and with our fellow human beings in like manner, let us learn to treat and respect mother nature as it will be profitable to all humanity and animal life instead of digging ourselves into an early grave. If we don't respect nature and continue to abuse her, she is not going to respect us either! If we don't engage in seeking out faith and spirit and learning to be in tune with them in our hearts and minds, we will derail from the principal aspect of maintaining a well balanced morally good and a healthy life.

Everything around us is deteriorating and it is going to be very difficult for the generations to come to live in a world been depleted of its natural resources. This is of a major importance. We are to correct, manage and control first our secret place occupants, that is our spirit and soul, than our hearts and minds, than our bodies, our relations with fellow human beings, nature and our own loved ones and all for a better legacy to be left behind to the next generation. Just living according to the flesh and our carnal mind or the ways of this world trends is never and has never been the resolve for a better future, come what may.

Teenagers

On a cold, windy and raining day, my best friend Luca told me that his brother Joseph had died in a car accident. It was already a dull and miserable day, and all I needed was to hear this bad news. He was only in his early twenties, full of energy and plans for his future, with a long life ahead of him been so sadly and abruptly cut short. We grew up together, went to the same school, lived in the same village, met with the same group of friends which we used to hang around with, laughed together and cried together. Luca and Joseph had left our village, some 5 years before any of us did, to go and work in the city and make a life and a future there for themselves. By the time Joseph died, Luca was married with one of our local girls while Joseph married a city girl. A little young to marry some would say in our parts, maintaining the old grandparents traditions, meaning, get a job first, secure it and don't let it go, save money to put towards a mortgage and buy only what you can afford, get a good hard working and faithful wife/husband and have children to pass it all on. This is the culture I grew up with and find it to be still so back at home. Every place, town or city, has its own beliefs and differences from else where, as some marry in their late twenties or thirties and some sooner. Living in the city has many distractions and a different kind of pace and lifestyles compared to that of our small town.

A typical teenage day out, back home in Minori, which is a small village situated in the south of Italy, would be to get together after school, having first done our homework, and than go out and play a little football or basketball game, or learn new skills in private tuition or getting together with friends. Many are traditionally geared in learning how to play musical instruments as there is always a demand for young musicians to join the many local bands whom are fairly busy throughout the year taking part in musical evenings to entertain the general public and to celebrate the numerous festive days, supported by the local mayor and council. During the summer, when the opportunity presented itself, we would go swimming in the day and many at times in the warm evenings, followed by singing Beatles songs accompanied by Andrea's guitar and we would fill the air with laughter often breaking out in a loud chorus, entertaining the holiday makers as they passed by, who would come from all over the world and visit our beautiful enchanting village. Many evenings were often filled with us eating pizzas and drinking Coca Cola's all around and watermelon to finish it off. In the winter times, when it wasn't raining, we would be doing pretty much the same things except eating watermelon or go for a swim, still using the beach as our favourite place to hang out and this came to be our second home. When it was particularly windy or cold to stay on the sandy beach we would retreat to other inland spots which we knew to be not so crowded in order that we could have total freedom with the place all for ourselves.

Our friends who moved to a city, told us that the pace of life was hectic the minute you left your lodgings. More traffic, more people, more distractions, more not so good things to do, more places to go, more bars, more discos and fancy ballrooms, more girls and more money to spend. But with that also came, more alcohol consumption, more drugs, more sex and more dangers, more avenues and ways to go down a wrong path, with more temptations, more wolves ready to lure you in the wrong things and make a fast buck out of you or worse, the list was endless. If anyone wanted to go to a beach, the nearest seaside would be hours away, whether travelling by car or bus. When one is finding themselves alone in a big city and unfamiliar with the surroundings and the people around them, unless they use their wit and wise judgment, they can be the victims of rouge villains and these often use girls to lure a man in their nets. Two friends together is always better then one alone.

Smoking cigarettes, was a new dare in our young circle of friends and it started to creep in our midst with Luca and Joseph, later it was Marco and later still Lorenzo, but the rest of us would not succumb to their peer pressure to try and smoke, besides, it was an expensive habit to take on board and bad for our health too. The very bitterly cold winter days did not stop us from going out, and once every two to three weeks, we often organised meet ups to go and eat something in the evenings at one of the local pizzeria somewhere, or end up in someone's relative empty household and have a feast. We would be cooking pasta with bolognese sauce followed by sausages and greens, wine and a cake to close the evening off. During those food and drinking memorable times, we would erupt in such crazy humorous jokes that some of us began to audio record our fun episodes and later have even more fun playing the recordings back to ourselves and listening to each one of us teasing and making fun of each other. These were the simple but much enjoyed fun times of when we were growing up together in the safety net of our village, and it was with exciting expectations that we would arrange and meet in those occasions. We looked forward to spend time together and pass the time away in good company.

Summer school holidays

The school holiday summer months (yes it is months in Italy, three to be precise) were so anticipated by most of us except one or two, as these few had to go to work, helping their parents with their business, and I was one of those. For me it was a torture to see my friends enjoying the school holidays doing nothing but having leisure time, swimming and playing on the crowded beach with ball games, eating ice cream and drinking cool drinks while I would be slaving away under the hot weather working hard with my dad, and although he gave me a small amount of money once a month it didn't do any justice to the loss of my free time which all my other friends had. It wasn't all doom and gloom for me, for as much as I didn't enjoy working with dad I did learn a lot about being responsible and self disciplined from the early age of eleven years old. Many were the times in which we faced uncertain working days due to the weather changes. In those three months, every year, and from the age of eleven to sixteen years old I watched my dad making sacrifices to support me, my sister, mum, the rented shop premises they run to sell fish and paying the mortgage for the

fourth floor apartment we lived in. There were days that we didn't catch anything or very little and on those occasion it was work and pay, meaning, all the petrol used for our trip and all the bait we purchased was wasted, giving us no returning profit.
So, every summer, dad used to wake me up in the middle of the night to get myself dressed and ready for going to work, fishing with him. Mum and dad raised us up managing a fresh fish shop, dad catching fishes and mum selling them and when the weather was not good and too rough for us to go fishing, I would usually end up helping in the shop while my sister who was three years older than me, looked after things at home. Our fishing boat trips were long and we would go out in the dark Mediterranean sea, with one oil lamp and one electric light on the boat mast which was connected to the engine electric switches and battery. In those early hours of the morning, ranging from one am to three am, we would see many sea-scattered small lights from other fishing boats and every boat would go out for a few hours till the very early rise of the sun and begin fishing in the deep waters using long nylon lines with hooks and baits attached and small stones tied to this long lines to help the baits go down into the deep sea waters. We did not use nets, as our boat was not big enough or equipped to fish using the huge fishing nets the larger trawling boats use. We would go so far out that we could no longer see the land we had left behind.

The most beautiful sight which made me think seriously and deeply about nature, which we so easily take for granted, was watching the sun rising far in the horizon for the first time, it felt so close but the wonder of it all soon wore off as I watched that sight everyday. Fishing is a long and laborious work and time would be passing by fast and we usually returned on our beach in the early evenings, say between five to six pm. Back at home, I would be so tired that I would eat something and go straight to sleep, before doing it all over again the next day. Our food was usually a roll or two of bread with any filling plus some fruit and a bottle of water. Dad would not waste any working day or time in summer, as we worked seven days a week and even during festivity days of traditional celebrations, and I suppose my dad did this to make the most use of my help (every little helps) and my free time from school.

At sea I experienced hostile weather conditions and scary close up encounters with very large fish. I am talking whales that could have sunk us with one nudge of their heads or a sweep of their tail, our boat wasn't bigger then 6 to 7 meters in length and about two meters wide and one and a half meter deep. I got in touch with my inner man from a very young age, fearing and rejoicing, worrying and battling through all sorts of weathers, high seas, lack of sleeping hours and constant hard work. I had to learn to use my will over my body reactions and overcome my fears, emotions, feelings and weaknesses with my inner man, by leaning on hope, trusting my dad expertise and think positively and for the best, come what may. Many at times when the bad weather would suddenly be upon us, with waves splashing against our boat and the rain from above, I would end up frantically using a bucket to get the excess sea water from our boat. The first time we caught a shark, my dad used a long pole with a sharp hook attached and with it he would hook the fish and pull it inside the boat while the shark would be twisting and resisting being taken out of the sea water. Once in the boat the shark would still be moving like crazy and from side to side, so dad would bash him on the head with a large piece of wood to kill it, before he bit us. After many blows the shark stopped moving and I thought it was dead. But my dad to show me that he was still alive even in that state got a long wooden pole and placed this near the shark's mouth and immediately the shark bit it locking it in his jaws. I could not believe it, after having been subjected to so many blows and with his eyes out of his sockets, yet he was still alive enough to give as good as he got. Another time we went out tuna fishing, and when dad caught a large one, a real battle between dad and the fish begun. My dad could not handle the pulling strength of this fish, every time he managed to get the tuna near the boat he would energetically pull the line and swim away again, winning over my dad. Dad had to tie the rope fishing line to the boat to get the tuna tired and whenever the tuna stopped pulling away, my dad would restart to pulling him in, this went on for about an hour. Then at one point as the tuna fish got tired and allowed dad to get him very close to our boat, about a meter away, the tuna did a mighty jump out of the water and as he did this, at the same time, my dad gave a vigorous pull inward the boat and this large tuna, the same size of my dad's tall body frame, five feet and eleven inches, landed on my dad and both of them down into the boat floor. He was a huge fish and if he hadn't jumped out of the water my dad would have never been able to get him into the boat.

Once we went sword fishing and what a surprising day it turned out to be, as we caught so many of them that our boat was full, and we had to wear our Wellington boots on our feet to avoid been injured by their swords. It was a very unique day never to be repeated again. It really felt as if we had struck gold.

Many at times, Dad would disclose to me stories from his youth years at sea, some were fascinating to listen to and some were very sad, as people he knew lost their lives when their boats capsized in bad weather. My dad lived during the second world war and had also tales to share from those dreadful days, weeks, months, when he would be dealing with the American and English navy soldiers and exchange with them his many packets of cigarettes for their tins of corn beef and spam ham, bars of chocolate and biscuits. Dad said that our village was on bread rations and no other kind of food was available to us, the roads had many soldiers with road blocks and I suppose these were somehow preventing the food supplies coming through or they were taking it for themselves, who knows. War is always messy, horrible, cruel, selfish, unpredictable, and downright careless in harming one another, killing etc. During the war dad said that going fishing was out of the question as there were war planes above them and navy fleets patrolling the sea, firing at one another, bombing and shelling each other. Dad said that although food was in short supplies they had a large stock of tobacco to trade. This turned out to be a very fair and happy exchange were both parties, soldiers and villagers, benefited from one another when opportune times allowed this exchange of blessings to take place.

Dad saw many planes been hit by artillery fire and come down crashing into the sea waters, as English, Americans, Germans and Italians continued to fight in the war. He went on to say that when planes came down into the waters, he and the other fisherman's would go out with their boats to see what they could salvage, risking their lives. In the process of doing this they would end up saving soldiers lives and as many men as they could rescue preventing them from drowning. Only God knows what lies beneath these sea waters from all those battles of the past.

Back to the days I was working with dad, every two to three weeks, due to our fishing lines getting twisted and mangled we finally would have a brake from the boat work, and dad would be busy unravelling all the fishing lines, hooks and all, which often would get in that messy state by larger fishes, who would swim from one line towards another. Having sorted out the lines he would then place these evenly in a circle movement and laying them inside wood boxes, each box contained about three to four hundred meters length of line with about one hundred and fifty to two hundred hooks tied to it at intervals of every three meters and hooked on a cork rectangle shaped piece attached to the front of the wood box, so to not get entangled with the line itself, a very long time consuming task, and this was the only chance I had to take a break from the battering of sea fishing work, but still I would be asked to help him with all the line equipment sorting, more often then not. Sometimes it took a couple of days to prepare the fishing lines for the next fishing boat trip and when possible I would be allowed to stay at home and catch up on lost precious sleep and later, much later, when I would wake up, I would be disorientated, not knowing what day it was nor the time, often having slept twelve hours or more straight.

In the first two weeks that I went to work with dad fishing, I was sea sick and would vomit every day, this was the most awful experience for me, and dad would just say to me, you will be fine soon, a week or two and you will get used to the boat movement and you will never feel or be sea sick again, he was right, but still, it took two weeks for me to get past that vomiting initial recurring mess which I hated, and finally be settled. Mum was always against dad taking me with him at such a young age, just eleven years old. I dreaded being rudely awakened in the middle of the night, no matter how nice or softly my dad spoke to me, shaking with his huge hand the whole of my body, but I think he was desperate for help and for company too, even from a boy as young as I was, it made a huge difference to him. The bait my dad used on each hook lines was fresh anchovies or sardines. When summer was over, due to the school attendance, I was free again to spend time with my friends in the evenings. We had a lot to catch up with, and in the meantime we were growing up in each individual character and likes, some liked art, some music, some photography, some liked cooking and some were just looking to start work in any sector. University was out of the question, but small short courses at colleges of the chosen trade were much in our to do list, with the plan to then work our way up into whatever opportunity and area of business was available. Down our parts of the Amalfi coast, the catering industry is a big sought after employment road, and it attracts young and older male and female workers which are always in demand, and a good seventy per cent of teenagers seek and get employed in this sector, in neighbouring towns and cities. It has always been a seasonal work and rarely all year around. But thanks to the exposure on the internet and the web photos and videos, our villages, which are spread about all along the Amalfitan coast, have caused a worldwide free advertising campaign which has turned out to be very fruitful, and in the last 8 years, it has increased the incoming flow of the holidaymakers so much so that the catering industry is really booming, with many more people finding and getting work, as the bars, restaurants, hotels and any other smaller food outlets are doing very good business and for a good nine to ten months of the year, with a steady smaller amount of people coming over even during the winter months, whereas and before the internet, it was just six months of the year. This increase of Holidaymakers has also launched another lucrative business in all the south of Italy coastline, and that is to let apartments, bed and breakfast places which are springing up everywhere, as everyone wants a slice of the action and get on the ladder of letting out a place and make some extra money. Every apartment and bed and breakfast is competing with one another in prices, beautiful locations and views, and all the latest and modern facilities needed to stand out above the rest and get the customers. Ratings are also much in demand to impress the next occupier.

Looking for work

Back in my teenage years living in a small village had it's plus and minuses, work was thin on the ground as our predecessors took all the best jobs that came up for the taking and would be fast holding on to these. Since too many people were going after any available position, a good percentage of us youngsters begun to look for work elsewhere, depart and leave either to find work in a city or going abroad altogether. Only very few stayed at home. Those of us who where living abroad would regularly return home for a summer break, once or twice a year. Once again we would meet up and divulge in long conversations, talking things over a beer or two and spill the beans about what everyone has been up too, we would often discover the untold stories of the loss of more friends due to more car accidents, more drug related deaths, marriage and relationship breakdowns and so on. First friend we lost to a fatal accident was Gianni, as he fell from a high wall which he was descending down a drain pipe. Then we got the news of Franco, who died from a drug overdose, aged 18, then of our friend Mario who died when he got run over, then our dear friend Luca, the brother of Joseph, who died from drug abuse, leaving behind his wife and children. Years later, two other friends of ours died due to drug abuse, while others are still alive and settled with work and families in the north parts of Italy. In the last ten years we lost more of our friends due to ill health issues, their age ranged between their thirty's to fifty's years old. A few friends have actually returned to the village life, leaving the cities and nations behind, for good. They have often said the same thing; living in the city and working abroad you earn more money but you end up spending more money too because everything is more costly, such as going out for a meal or go to the cinema, or get that drink, buy fresh vegetables and fruit, get your laundry done or use the public transport.

When we were together all of us in our younger days, we felt secure, we were happy and worry free, for me these were the best years of our lives. Then, when we eventually grew up and became adults our youth has been lost and almost forgotten, for we all have our families, work and responsibilities that wipe out the few memories we had left of an era that is no more. Today in this generation things have changed so much that is hard to keep up with all the fast and progressive advances of electronic devices, the web and the media traffic on the net through which everyone streams in day and night. Years ago it would have been unthinkable to have a telephone in your hand all day long, a phone that allows you to tap in and find out about all the latest news in the world, gather any information you seek, take pictures and videos, watch movies and what have you. Many children as young as seven or eight years old already have one of these personal mobile phones. It is the modern craze beside gaming on a screen as well as the phones and books that can be read at the click of a button etc. Of course and naturally, anything that attracts so much attention from innumerable users worldwide is going to be a blessing for some and a cursing for others, it will enrich the world with good things, particularly in schools, colleges and universities, but also bad things. Many use the internet to make honest money and many use it to steal money, and the list of fraudulent ways and tactics used is a mile after mile long, driven and masterminded by dishonest and crooked people, who really don't care who is going to suffer, whether a single mother or a single father or a lonely widow or widower, already afflicted by restricted body mobility and little care.

Nowadays thieves have mellowed their ways and instead of the usual breaking into premises which still occurs, they have adapted and learned how to upgrade, making good use of this new technology to steal, kill and destroy the lives of many innocent people. They have also caused wars and disruption to many electrical computerised companies, breaking into these devices which are in control of homes, cars, vehicles of all sizes, communities, political and military bodies, economy and educational systems, humanitarian laws and what have you almost everywhere causing huge problems, losses, and chaos. All of these have affected banks and peoples accounts, robbing them of large sums from their savings with false promises and presentation of fake products wiping out credibility integrated in all the underlining structure of money laundering. This scumming epidemic has reached incredible heights, with a very lucrative band of computer hackers and charlatans, imposters, deceivers and cheaters, double dealers, phoney con men and con artist, that use with constant improvements today's technology to be chief money laundering experts laughing all the way to the bank and into many peoples accounts, virtually stealing people identities. The majority of the population in the general everyday affairs of this generation has gone money crazy, greedy and insatiably cunning in order to obtain as much money and assets as possible, dreaming and wishing for a life of self pampering to get all they want at any cost. It is frightening when looked from the opposite direction, you can never satisfy the continuous hunger of the flesh and carnal mind, which is dominated by the soul. The more they get the more they want and it is never enough to really satisfy their cravings, while the desires and demands they place upon themselves are continuously draining them of energy. It seems that everybody aspires to get on the booming property ladder. Construction of housing has skyrocketed to new heights with developers seeking to buy out more and more land and larger homes which are going to be demolished and replaced by building apartments with as many floors as they can get away with and make thousands of pounds in profit. No small empty place available which is up for the taking is left untouched, but quickly bought and fenced in, secured and ready for demolition and more building work of flats and apartments will soon follow. Society has been caught in this whirlwind of money making, bombarded by adverts, television programs, seminars, internet strategies where everyone wants a slice of it all and get rich, for that is what they entice everyone to do, get rich and you will be well and happy. Money is important to some because they desperately are in need of it, whilst to others is just a means to live in a more luxurious lifestyle, more of this and more of that, which never really satisfies.

The secret place

What has a secret place got to do with all this? In short and to the point I have this secret place, you have it, and everybody has it, we all carry it inside of us but what is it and what are we hiding, what are we storing in it and for what purpose and why is it so secretive? Our spirit and soul, heart and mind, determines our decisions, how strong or how weak we get charged to the get up and go, do this and do that, drive here and drive there, answer or not answer to provocations, to opportunities that are so important or not so important, all these will contribute in shaping our days ahead, the way we get a good night rest or we don't, the state of our physical well being, learning how to be content and at peace, enjoying this blissful state and do not allow anything from the outside to permeate in our inside with all its dirt, which will inadvertently build cobwebs trapping more dirt and unfamiliarity that goes on unseen but later on felt. Have you ever heard the famous saying: You are what you eat? Well I want to add to this saying my own one: "You become what you spend most time with". Most of what we tend to hide is not spoken of, not telling anyone and locking it safely away from everybody's sight. Our secret place is well hidden into this wonderful and multitalented but complicated body of ours. We can be very open and reveal the most secrets of the heart or we can securely lock them in there by keeping our mouth shut to its contents, but however and whatever we will manage to keep hidden, we will still be ending up showing, disclosing and revealing to others all that we securely hide away. How? By our actions, bad habits, words, character, temperament, self control or the lack of it, being short tempered, stressful, unsettled, overworked, overstretched, confused and overall being moody, in negative mode or picking and moaning on everyone except oneself. Does any one remember or recognise all of these or just some? Many believe that we are just a body made of flesh, bones and blood, but the reality is that we are also spiritual beings at all times, wherever we go, whatever we do or think and say, or don't do or think or say. We can be awake or asleep it doesn't matter, our spiritual self, our consciences are all active and alive, they are living just as we breathe and we can either help these function correctly or afflict them to such an extent that they will take years away from us and bring in bad health. Our decisions and our actions are to be guided and used with careful management so that we can help ourselves from the moment we wake up to the moment we go to sleep, and adding and contributing a disciplined pace and path that leads to our well being and that of others around us. Slowing down, being consistent, enduring and persevering in acquiring knowledge and understanding of how our body works, are just some of the qualities that go hand in hand for the contents of our secret place to add years to our lives and not rob us or deplete ourselves of them.

When we are formed in our mothers womb our spiritual side is growing within us too, encased in our souls, hearts and minds and although they seem to be functioning all together in agreement they are actually different from one another. Of course, no medical machinery in existence can ever see our spirit and soul for they are only visible to the realm from which they come from, originated by like manner matter and essence, strength and life, intellect and feelings. But there are medical machines that can monitor and detect mind activity in rising or lowering. Depending in the way we have lived or are living, the environment we have been brought up in, the life and the experiences of it, a very hectic present life or a very easy one, or something in between, it all affects us physically and mentally but also spiritually, in many different ways and levels. If we get very weary and tired from excessive work, long hours, and lack of sleep, we are not only depleting our physical body parts but we are exhausting and pushing far ahead and headlong into the foreground our spirits also, which are going to be suppressed and trampled upon from all that we shouldn't be doing. Have you fallen into the habit of having another cup of coffee, (usually ending up with having one too many) each time you are feeling been drained away of energy? I know of many people who have six cups of coffee a day and some even seven cups. This is far too much caffeine which is pushing the body clock into overdrive and it will affects the sleeping pattern and eventually the physical clock will go haywire, then the romantic side of us will have gone, the conversations will suffer, our friends and loved ones who called or sent an email or a text message on your mobile, don't get answered for days, weeks and even months whilst the relationships begins to dysfunction somewhat, your other daily tasks and family and friends undoubtedly will start getting out of order, out of control and out of sight, and all one is left with is themselves dealing with themselves, even when they are living in a house with their siblings and parents, grandparents or just sharing with friends or strangers, or you are married with kids but still feel you are on your own whilst living in their company.

It is at this stage that many without knowing why, begin to turn to alcohol or gambling, or some other habit like secretly injecting with drugs and substances, getting deeper into a spiral of immoral actions, flirting with the uncertain and meddling with fire. Why fire? Because too many tap into all these wrong things instead of slowing down, instead of been happy with less, instead of taking care of their sleeping pattern, and food and drink intake, because all these things matter more that those extra hours at work. Relationship with others, particularly our own families, matter more than not bothering or making the time. Time is very precious to all of us, how we use it and for whom or what as it makes life go round, virtually. Many have got used to eating another bar of chocolate to keep them going further along the hours of their working schedule, then two hours later they will have a cake and so on, this has caused a worldwide epidemic of Diabetes, both type one and type two, and I tell you, this is related to stress, overeating, over drinking all the wrong things. Adding to all this is the lack of sleeping hours, the worries, the higher mortgage, the bills not paid on time, and so much more that it is no wonder people are dying of so many illnesses in their younger years then ever before. I also know of many people who use drugs and other harmful substances not just to work longer hours but to do many other things in their life, just like people who wake up in the morning and instead of drinking tea they are drinking alcoholic drinks. These descriptions are manifested in full view everywhere throughout this earth, and many teenagers have succumbed to drug and alcohol abuse, leaving behind their grieving parents and siblings, girlfriends and boyfriends, all for keeping up with these vicious worldly trends, that always seem to be so harmless but in reality are masking the real damaging strength that accompanies them to steal lives, kill lives and destroy them.

So, for all the overbearing long and extra working hours to get a bigger house or more money for more holidays, people become victims of their own actions, and for these reasons all sorts of things come up in our daily chores, like a sudden headache, an ache or pain into our side or belly or back, or legs, and what do we do? We run to the doctor for this prescription and that cure, fooling ourselves that this is going to solve the physical problems, well it won't do that, but what it will do is cause side effects to an already overtired, overstressed, overworked, over abused, and neglected spiritual and physical body which will keep going on a confusion road of mayhem and madness not detected till it is too late.

So why it is not detected? Because when a body is in such a state it is human nature to react in stubbornness, fear, doubt, been overbearing and over proud, high and mighty, arrogant and cocky, lying to oneself, when on the other hand, someone who sees what the person in question does not see, is trying to get them to see it too but instead they choose to reject the good advice reacting wrongly, when really and in truth they are lacking in knowledge and wisdom for the things that are spiritual. We are to be very careful because in the spiritual realm there are good spirits and bad ones, which in turn affect our spirits from one or the other and in all the way mentioned so far in this book, which can tip a person over the cliff so to speak or into a safe journey of recuperation, re-energising, refreshing the inner parts with proper rest and detoxification and to break free from the enslaving tie that is shackling them presenting a no way out when in reality the way out is there for the taking all the time, but either there is no willingness to escape from it all or the invisible rope is so tight that one is not able to break free from it and is really in need of some help.

Usually the person becomes caught in the motion of their own spinning wheel, that they are in charge of their own body, and ignoring the warning signs from within and from those who tell them in good stead, meaning well wishes for them, they become blind to it all, spirit, soul and body. What will benefit our body is a healthy carefully selected and natural food diet, proper rest and a just lifestyle. This will remove all the junk and dirty cobwebs from our well designed body functions allowing our spiritual side to breathe with a different pace of life and proper and adequate rest, good moral living, not being passive but actively going about treating others as we would like others to treat us, instead it seems and looks like, that we have progressed and become used to wanting, receiving and gaining only but not so much giving or helping others in whatever way one can. This two different and opposing ways of life either harbour all kinds of ills or all kinds of benefits in our secret place which has always been there unseen, untouched but somehow filled with either blessings for us or ill intentions, negative thoughts spiralling into actions, often producing low self esteem, depression, discouragement, sickness or other. Most unwanted problems begin to affect our health and our present and future peace, our serenity, joy, gladness and good health, our relationships with our loved ones and others. All of these stem forth from storing fears, doubts, uncertainties, bad judgement, unrighteousness, bad habits, spending hours a day watching the wrong kind of things, listening to the wrong things, all of which will come out of us one way or another, whether good or bad, becoming exposed for all to see in numerous other ways. What goes in must come out. What I mean is that what we watch and listen to, gets into our soul and spirit, and it begins to accumulate and take so much room that there won't be space for anything else. What we spend time with, that it is what we become.

How many times has someone done something which the inner spirit rings alarm bells as risky or wrong to be followed through, yet, one still goes ahead and does it anyway because it feels good or is their desired intention and decision to do so. If we do not feed our secret place with the right food the right and just motives sooner or later it will affect our spirit which will become oppressed no end, and what we store in there it is also what is going to come out. For example lets take a young couple going on a ladder to purchase their first property, They have enough budget to get a one bedroom house, but end up going for a double bed one, even so it is out of their budget, as they have looked with more desire to the bigger place, and begin to think that they can do more hours at work and save more money to pay a mortgage of say 25 years. But you see they have ignored the secret place warning signs of wisdom which is encrypted in them and they have overridden these by delightfully indulging in quenching their worldly and fleshly desire, which in turns gets them to lose important resting hours and lack of sleep, social time will suffer and so on, piling pressure on themselves and their inner-selves, losing their peace, accommodating stress, which in turn brings on illness often accompanied by quarrels which in turn leads to cause frictions and lack of trust and love for one another, blaming each other and in anger and frustration and due to lack of self control one or both of them walks into unfaithfulness, adultery and finally divorce. Adultery is at the top of the list as the most causes for a divorce.

Picture a very common scene where there comes the temptation to overspend, perhaps get an overdraft and overindulging in food and drink in tapas bars and restaurants leaving with an hefty bill to pay, the desire for a bigger and more expensive car is usually number two on the list of things to get, straight after the property purchase, and all of this is not going to help such a couple, which ought to think first and foremost for their bodies wholeness, well-being and also guard their spiritual side, but in all honesty, no one even believes that they are also spiritual let alone give a thought to it, and therefore they end up draining and abusing their inner selves and at some point they will inevitably pay the costly price, of doctors, a cupboard full of medicine, hospital attendances, operations and much worse. We are built this way and we are to seriously take note and be more aware that there is a balance to be implemented between these two, the carnal body and the spiritual inner body. Beside this there is the all ruling inner soul that tries to dominate and be in charge of whatever the balancing scale will tip on, in the spirit, or in the carnal wordily unrighteous ways and here lies the rise and or fall of any of us. Our souls are in charge of our feelings, desires, emotions, which will also control our minds and consequently our actions, our words and reactions, our holding back from speaking and our lashing out in anger or be sporadically abusive, getting drunk, trying out drugs, becoming addicted to this or to that etc. For some there is a drastic turn around towards a good and moderate self controlled lifestyle, saying no when it needs to be said no and yes when it needs to be a yes. But until we learn to overcome and keep in check our soul it will control us instead.

Our grandparents in our village, lived a much healthier and longer peaceful life than we do today and they never lacked food, drink or accommodation, they were simply happy with what they got and with what they had, and they didn't miss anything nor did they make too many visits to see the doctor. Blood pressure was non existent to them. They were at peace with their slower pace of life, getting enough sleep at night and getting up early in the mornings well refreshed, rested and energised, and in their inner secret place all was in accord and agreement, functioning at the same level of simplicity, eating, working, resting and playing.

All those friends of mine who indulged in drugs and a hectic lifestyle of chasing women, drinking, fast living and harbouring the wrong things within ended up having more waking up hours during the day and less sleeping hours at night and their health and spirits suffered till their body clockwork gave up on them. They did not know that their spirit was dying as it placed forceful demands on the body and weakening the immune system, which in turn deteriorated the capacity of the lymph nodes system, which placed confusion in the body good cells and the blood pressure and circulation, which causes the mind to dive into unrest and overworked chaos, and whilst their bank account was better than the one who lived at a much lower pace, these faired better in getting enough work and adequate sleep, lived a longer and happier life, while on the other hand, those with the larger savings, had to spend what they had accumulated in medical bills and the result of many was prolonged sickness and later early death. These are the repercussions of overworking and ignoring the sustenance and provisions needed for guarding our secret place, our hearts content. What are our daily thoughts like? Our thoughts determine our actions, therefore if a person is constantly thinking about earning more money or how to find a happy, they are inclined to walk over everything and everyone in order to do so. A peaceful and stress free healthy mind will be geared to make steps and decisions towards a happy medium between being rich or be satisfied, and making the most of what one already has. Are you seeking a bigger house, a luxury holiday, two cars or two homes instead of one, and after getting that, desire to want some more? If yes, you have fallen into the trap of the worldly ways and damaging your spiritual self.

I hear many say; so what's wrong with wanting more of whatever? I would reply and say that more money and pleasures can't buy you good happy and stable health in later life, for too many who have abused their inner and outer selves have gone and departed from this earth too soon. Money, no matter how much you have of it, can't buy you health, and rich and wealthy people have died and before dying they have confessed, admitted and concluded, that all the money they made served them absolutely nothing, especially when they needed it to work and perform for them, it didn't, not even with the best doctors, surgeons and medicines in the world. Do we see right here that money can't buy us the most important thing in our life? Or is life not so important at that. Some will scoff at all of this, but some have regretted the way they lived ignoring all the warning signs till it was too late. Who wants to lose a dad or a mum, a brother or a sister, a son or a daughter, a husband or a wife, a friend or a relative, when they could have prevented it or helped in preventing it? At times it is the wrong decision been made that spirals someone towards early death, at other times it is fate, being in the wrong place at the wrong time, at other times is a sickness affecting the weaker body immune system, while for others who are built with a stronger immune system and exposed to the same virus, infection or other, have come out untouched and unaffected compared to the other person.

Some say that their sickness is genetic. There are many reasons, options, debates and controversial discussions to include in this subject, but it is to be said that it is also true and a fact that pushing, shoving and stressing our bodies will eventually catch up on us and not in a good way. Abusing our bodies with earthly substances will abuse our spiritual system at the same time and this goes also for unrighteous thinking and actions, unjust, wicked or perverse stimuli actions as such will defile us from the inside to the outside. As it is often spoken and heard a guilty consciousness will eat away at your spirit and soul, disrupting the harmonious natural inner senses and calm.

We are to take care of ourselves both inwardly and outwardly, striking a good balance of a decent healthy and happy lifestyle, and not to hide or accumulate in our secret place all the stress all the wanting all the distractions and temptations that surround us, we are to resist these as fast as they come our way when we see the warning light switching itself on from amber to red. As I mentioned before, ignoring these inner warnings will lead us into a spiral of consequences that will be virtually undetected in its beginning forms, but will creep silently and grow within and suddenly go full force forward, passing right by our spirits and souls, crashing them, suppressing our energy resources already weighed down by fatigue, worries, fears, wrongdoings, lying, having a grudge or two, raving in gossiping and moan and grumble about all sorts of things. All of these will deplete and suffocate our natural inner defences so much so that we lose hope, we lose a stable mental functioning, we lose self control and the ability to fight, we lose our joy for if we lose the fight from within we will never win the fight outwardly, it will give up and slowly shutting its defences down, no matter what we take or where we go.

Like a computer just before suddenly crashing, so it is with us, spirit, soul and body to an early death. This book is not to be applied to every case of death but within the writing contents there is a good indication of certain death's to why they occur and to what is their causes. My intention is to confirm and reaffirm what most people already know but choose to ignore when things are going good, till they will hit an invisible wall, which unfortunately for us does exists and it is felt within and the impact is not in any way pleasant, be it an heart attack, fainting in the middle of the street or lose consciousness whilst driving a vehicle or fall asleep at the wheel etc. I have actually witnessed these very things.

The solution to what has been shared is all going on within our hearts contents, in our spirit and souls chambers and is called the most secret place in every human being on earth. Secret because we keep it so and do not like to expose it for all too see, secret because we are embarrassed of the things we have said and done, secret because there are constructions going on outside which stem from within in greed and in wanting much more then what we have, secret because we are never satisfied, secret because we have realised to have acted wrongly and the guilt goes on growing and stirring us in the wrong directions causing us to feel a mix of regret and hatred which unsettles the spirit further, secret because we have told too many lies and hurt too many people in the process, secret because we want to glory in our name, secret because we give in to jealousy and malice when we should really overcome these, secret because we run to the wrong places and to the wrong people, getting ourselves in worse situations from when or where we started to look for a solution to our problems and getting deeper in the trouble zone of the physical and spiritual defects that will affect our performance in our every day tasks, secret because we didn't say no and said yes instead to certain things and certain people, secret for not doing what we should have done, and secret for doing what we shouldn't have done. This is not a riddle to confuse anyone it is simply what we often end up doing (or not), thinking and telling ourselves that nothing has happened when actually, we know deep inside something was not right or doesn't feel right, but it has already affected us in the spiritual self, and we do these things once, twice, three times and keep on doing them in a variety of ways, and at some point or another we become so used to doing such things that no longer it will be warning us mentally, so we think and say to ourselves, it is OK, I am in control, nothing bad will happen to me, it is just harmless fun, everybody is doing it, for so our mind will whisper to us, but by that time, when we do not care any more, come whatever it is we may have achieved or gained, the truth is we would have amassed so much inwardly wrongdoings and bad habits that nothing good will come out of us and if we prosper it will be due to dishonest gains rather then honest ones, and it will catch up and bleed into the spiritual side of us which by this time will be ceased up and dying leaving our bodies to follow suite. The highs will usually come before the lows, it will be an exiting time of euphoria when following the mind desires, and the more one feeds these the more they will want, and then it will hit releasing all the wrong emotions affecting the person inside as well as outside. We are what we eat but we are also what we do, for how long or how little. Too much salt will spoil the broth and is bad for us, not enough salt and the dinner will not be so tasty. So it is with our bodies, spirit, soul and mind.

We are to engage with these and be in touch and in harmony with them for a happy, long lasting medium, tipping the scales towards managing the contents of our hearts and the things we store in there. In sharing some things spiritual I can focus on the subject of Prayer. Do people, whether in a positive way or a negative one, speak about prayer? Do people actually believe in prayer and practice it in their life? Why do some people believe in it and some don't? What is prayer? This is a subject much discussed in our entire world and to all who believe and persevere in the act of prayer they can honestly admit that prayer is an action based on faith. What is faith? Faith is believing in something or someone that can't be seen or touched but yet is felt within our spirit, not always, but many at times through the course of our prayer lives. Faith is taking action in doing something with hope come what may and be prepared for any eventual outcome, meaning, one overcomes their fears, doubts or anxieties. When I was a young boy, like many other boys, I liked and enjoyed watching cowboys and Indian films with gunfighters such as John Wayne, Clint Eastwood and so many well known actors, and in many of these movies I saw both Indians and cowboys praying, but they did this only when they were in danger or facing a battle. Prayer, although expressed in words is originated from our spirit and soul, heart and mind, progressing with a bag full of intentions to help someone or ourselves for a better outcome in any given serious situation, or a difficult circumstance one will find themselves in. But for the real believers in prayer, it is a lifestyle, whether their prayer will get always answered or not, whether they receive a successful response only now and then or they don't, whether they are criticised or misunderstood for believing and acting upon prayer, and so on.

The experiences of prayer are all spiritually discerned and they are fuelled from within us to be released in words which are powered by faith for good moral things only, and I say this because the spiritual realm is populated by good and bad forces, powers and Dominions, unseen but sometimes visible to us. For example many people have seen angels, good ones and bad ones, and some of these eye witnesses are believed in what they say and some are not. I myself have actually seen the figure of an angel of light only once and in a church, and his outline was a very strong and brilliant light glowing luminously brighter then a light bulb. When I asked my wife who was sitting next to me if she could see the angel as I pointed my finger to show the spot where he was, she could not see anything, yet I could. When in prayer and calling upon the help from Holy angels, I have received their help with prayers answered even with the results taking place in distant countries, from one nation to another. I share this true event which unfolded when I attended a regular household prayer meeting. The house owners were a married couple with two grown up children, a boy and a girl. This couple were missionaries and he was a pastor too. It was one of those normal evenings when you just come together have tea or a coffee with some biscuits and after that begin to pray according to the pastor prayer requests. Every participant in those prayer meets believed in prayer and did it regularly.

That evening came forth this request from the Pastor; We have a missionary couple, friends of ours, who are spreading the good news of the Lord Jesus Christ in Ghana and they have two young boys, ages seven and eight, who attended the local school. Being a region where there is a lot of spiritual witchcraft activities, inadvertently once they find out the presence of anyone promoting the true help from the spirit realm, that is God, it becomes a threat to them for they know it is a very powerful source to contend with which can remove their lucrative but sinister dealings and works of their association with unclean spirits. So the pastor went on to explain that their missionary friends in Ghana, had their two boys in serious bad health so much so that they were dying due to a curse placed upon them. What happened was that some child gave their two boys a cake in the school break time, and since they ate it they became very sick, and their health continued to spiral downwards. In matter of several weeks and between Doctors and Hospital visits their children were deteriorating gradually each day, and the last news they received from them, was that the morning day of our prayer meeting they would take the children to hospital to die in there as they were lifeless and without energy, in fact they could not walk and one of the boys was already loosing consciousness in a delirious state as they spoke about it all. No doctor knew why they were so seriously ill and what kind or type of sickness was attacking their bodies, and they told the parents there is nothing more we can do, but the parents knew to use prayer and were asking for others to pray to lift the curse from the children.

In the evening prayer meeting, which was here in England, one by one said their prayers, I was the last one to pray and when it was my turn I spoke with righteous anger, in a loud voice, and I did not ask but I commanded to Holy angels that they would go immediately to these two boys, lift and remove for good the curse that was upon them, and destroy the works of witchcraft and dark spirits. None of the others had prayed with such zeal and so directly nor did they command holy angels in the manner I did. The evening ended as usual and everyone went home. Next morning I received a text message, it was from the pastor where I attended the evening prayer meeting, and he was saying that he had just then received news from Ghana regarding the two dying boys, they were discharged from the hospital that very morning as they did a remarkable and miraculous turn around from the early hours of the morning onwards. There was no medical explanation given except that a miracle had just taken place. I know that many have lost their loved ones in and during many prayers been said, but I also and honestly know and can affirm with my hand on heart that many prayers have also been answered and many have been made whole and well again, going from medical reports of no hope situations to hope and remarkable recovery. I myself, choose not to focus on the negative side of the spiritual realm but on the positive side of it, discarding the losses and stare in wonder at the victories obtained. Many are the true testimony of miracles, signs and wonders I have witnessed and heard from many of my praying friends and all due to the faith released in prayer.

Words have power and they can either help or hinder the manifestation taking place from the spiritual to the physical. The only way to find out if it is all true, is to begin to practice prayer, in faith, believing and praying to the Holy One God Almighty, the Creator of all things visible and invisible in the entire universe because He is the hearer and the interceptor of every prayer ever said, He judges and He does it righteously, we may not understand to why this and why that, because His ways and thoughts are not like our ways and thoughts, therefore His Spirit is way above ours, for He has said that as Heaven is higher than our earth so are His ways and thoughts higher than our ways and thoughts. This is written in the Bible in the Book of the Prophet Isaiah chapter fifty five and verse eight (55:8). I recall another evening prayer meeting in a different house were there was a projector playing a worship song for us all and we were reading the words projected on a wall and singing along if we wished. In the middle of the song the projector connected to a laptop just stopped and would not work. The house group leader tried several times to restart it all and was very disappointed that the machine would not sync or work with the computer. Unknown to everyone in there, when I arrived at the house and parked my car in their drive, I said a prayer saying: Lord Jesus, if there is anything you want me to do or say this evening, just let me hear You or see what You want me to see.

So while we were trying to sing from reading the written song on sheets of paper I suddenly just shouted very loudly as I pointed my finger at the projector and laptop, START! and as I said nothing more I heard in my spirit the words; "in Jesus name". As soon as I added the words "in Jesus name", the projector started to work again and was fine again. I was so excited and ecstatic at what had just happened that I started to jump up and down in the room touching the ceiling with my fingers and outstretched arms like a child who just scored his first goal in a game of football as everyone was just looking on smiling in bewilderment.

Another time I prayed in a house group for a lady whose leg was in pain and after I prayed all the pain left her immediately. Another time the house group leader asked me to pray for his bad back and as I did pray for him he said that something lifted off his back. Another lady testified that since I had prayed for her Lymphoid legs they have been really good. A man in another house group evening with a troubled stomach said that as I prayed he felt something leaving his belly. I have so many other occasions were prayer has achieved its purposes and delivered the goods so to speak. When one will try and pray for the first time it will feel like climbing a steep mountain, but if they will just speak one word here and one word there they will begin to gain ground, till more words will come, but if one does not start then it is just that, a non starter prayer. Prayer is the ignition key that sparks the spiritual realm engine on and begins to rev up till one puts it into fist gear, then second, then third gear and so on till they will get used to a smooth prayerful driving.

I hope to have stirred someone in the right direction of this one life we get in this world, with the understanding and perceptiveness of our inwardly self and the aforementioned complicated (or not) functioning of it all, the effects and the most likely results, may all who will have read this book read it again and do so with their heart and not just their head, applying a measure of faith and a voluntary willingness to try to connect with their inner self by giving a good solid and long lasting go. Believing and not disbelieving in our spiritual self is the first phase into the first chapter of our secret place, invisible it may be but is spiritually discerned and visible to us when we begin to see with the eyes of the heart. If we remain in awareness to this it will never be too late to start and choose to believe and to act on the basis of a favourable and capable wisdom born and sustained from within our spirits, for a better, more peaceful, content and satisfied joyful living with ourselves, our fellow human beings and the heavenly spiritual realm around us. The fight is good versus bad, spirit and soul, mind and body, as we are the only ones to make things happen and in a good way, from good thoughts and practice. The choices which we make today and tomorrow will determine the course of our lives from start to finish, from youth to adulthood and finally to good old age. We are multitalented, multi gifted and it is not of our own but a gift from God to us all in many different ways which need to be used and nurtured time and time again till our last, for our good and that of those who know us and are around us, near and far.

Blessings

Bonaventura Apicella

Printed in Poland
by Amazon Fulfillment
Poland Sp. z o.o., Wrocław